Smithsonian

LITTLE EXPLORER

My BODY

by Martha E. H. Rustad

CAPSTONE PRESS
a capstone imprint

Little Explorer is published by Capstone Press,
1710 Roe Crest Drive, North Mankato, Minnesota 56003
www.capstonepub.com

For Jared. —MEHR

Library of Congress Cataloging-in-Publication Data
Rustad, Martha E. H. (Martha Elizabeth Hillman), 1975-
 My body / by Martha E.H. Rustad.
    pages cm. — (Smithsonian little explorer)
 Audience: 4-8.
 Audience: K to grade 3.
 Summary: "Introduces basic anatomy to young readers,
including major systems and organs, health, and
safety"— Provided by publisher.
 Includes bibliographical references and index.
 ISBN 978-1-4765-0250-2 (library binding)
 ISBN 978-1-4765-3544-9 (paper over board)
 ISBN 978-1-4765-3550-0 (paperback)
 ISBN 978-1-4765-3556-2 (ebook PDF)
1. Human body—Juvenile literature. 2. Human
physiology—Juvenile literature. I. Title.
QP37.R86 2014
612—dc23   2012050592

Editorial Credits
Kristen Mohn, editor; Sarah Bennett, designer; Eric Gohl,
media researcher; Kathy McColley, production specialist

Our very special thanks to Don E. Wilson, PhD, Curator
Emeritus of the Department of Vertebrate Zoology at
Smithsonian's National Museum of Natural History,
for his curatorial review. Capstone would also like to
thank Kealy Wilson, Smithsonian Institution Project
Coordinator and Product Development Manager, and
the following at Smithsonian Enterprises: Ellen Nanney,
Licensing Manager; Brigid Ferraro, Director of Licensing;
Carol LeBlanc, Senior Vice President, Consumer &
Education Products.

Printed in the United States of America in Brainerd, Minnesota.
032013   007721BANGF13

Image Credits
BigStockPhoto.com: Studio1One, cover; Capstone: 7
(top), Becky Shipe, 8 (middle right & bottom right), 9
(top right), 10 (top left), 13, 14 (all), 16, 17 (top), 20, 21
(top right), 25 (middle & bottom), Brandon Reibeling, 8
(top right); iStockphotos: Josef Philipp, 9 (middle right);
Science Source: Biophoto Associates, 12 (middle left),
Ted Kinsman, 19 (bottom); Shutterstock: advent, 2–3,
Aleksandar Videnovic, 30, Andresr, 21 (left), Aprilphoto,
11, Cheryl Casey, 26 (left), 26–27, D. Hammonds, 7
(bottom), Daniel Korzeniewski, 5, Dimarion, 6 (right),
Fanfo, 25 (top), forestpath, 17 (bottom left), FotoBug11,
24, Fotokostic, 28–29 (top), gasa, 32, Hein Nouwens,
4 (top right), 5 (bottom), 15 (bottom), Katrina Brown,
27 (top right), KatarinaF, 28 (bottom), Kuttelvaserova
Stuchelova, 18 (top), Levent Konuk, 21 (bottom right),
Liunian, 1, Michael C. Gray, 10 (bottom), Monkey
Business Images, 8 (left), nemlaza, 9 (bottom right), 12
(bottom right), PanicAttack, 22 (top), Rob Marmion, 4
(top left), Sainthorant Daniel, 15, 29 (bottom), Samuel
Borges Photography, 9 (left), Stuart Monk, 22 (bottom),
Studio 1One, 18 (bottom), Suzanne Tucker, 12 (top
right), 19, Tatyana Vychegzhanina, 23, Vietrov Dmytro, 4
(bottom left), W.JARVA, 10 (top right), wavebreakmedia,
4 (bottom right), 6 (left), Yang Na, 17 (bottom right)

Design Elements: Shutterstock

TABLE OF CONTENTS

MY BODY

My body is an amazing machine.

It helps me learn and eat and play.

After high school doctors study for as long as 16 years to learn all about the body.

4

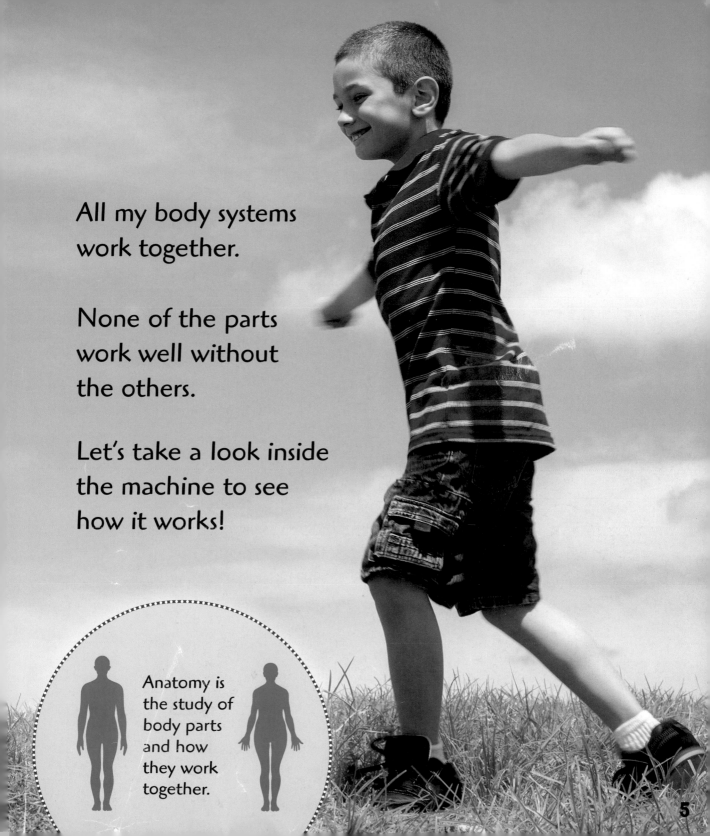

All my body systems
work together.

None of the parts
work well without
the others.

Let's take a look inside
the machine to see
how it works!

Anatomy is
the study of
body parts
and how
they work
together.

5

MY CELLS

Tiny cells make up my whole body.

Different kinds of cells make each part.

We can see cells only with a microscope.

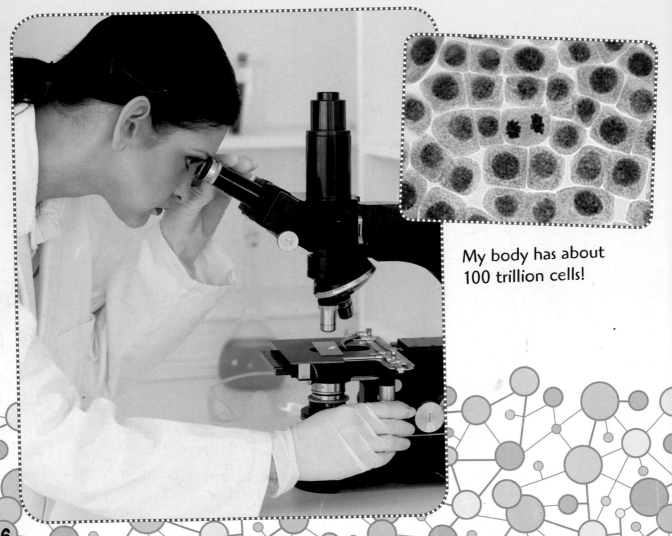

My body has about 100 trillion cells!

A CELL

CELL MEMBRANE
the outside layer
of a cell

NUCLEUS
a part of a cell
that controls it

CYTOPLASM
a liquid that
fills up a cell

Most of my body is made of water.
If I weigh 100 pounds (45 kilograms),
about 60 pounds (27 kg) is water.

MY SKELETON

Bones make up my skeleton.

My skeleton holds up my body and gives it shape.

X-RAY

My skull bones keep my brain safe. I wear a helmet when I ride my bike to keep my brain even safer.

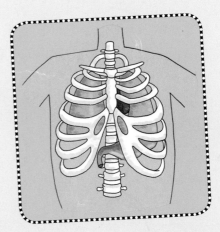

Some bones keep soft body parts safe.

Between my bones are joints.

Joints help my body move.

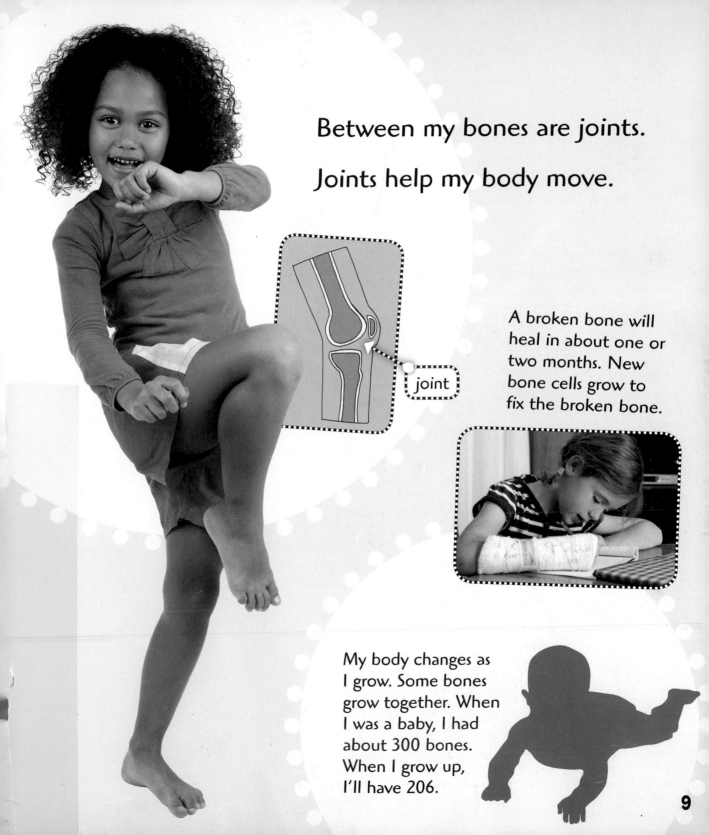

joint

A broken bone will heal in about one or two months. New bone cells grow to fix the broken bone.

My body changes as I grow. Some bones grow together. When I was a baby, I had about 300 bones. When I grow up, I'll have 206.

MY MUSCLES

Muscles help my body move.

Skeletal muscles pull on my bones.

arm muscle

arm bone

I move these muscles to keep them strong.

My body has 600 muscles.

Smooth muscles work even when
I don't think about them.

Some move food through my body.

Others help
me breathe.

MY BLOOD

Blood is a red liquid that travels through my body.

It brings nutrients to my body parts.

Blood carries away waste my body doesn't need.

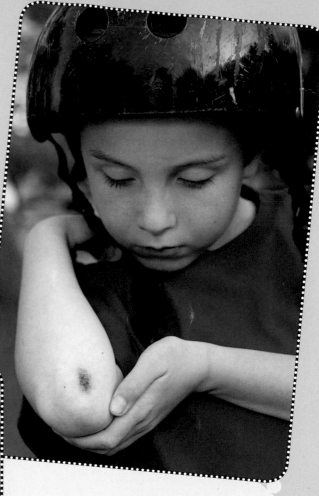

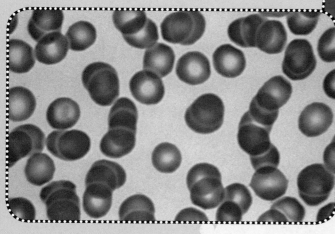

Red blood cells carry oxygen from the lungs to the rest of the body.

An adult's body holds about 21 cups (5 liters) of blood.

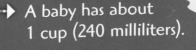

A baby has about 1 cup (240 milliliters).

Blood moves in narrow tubes.

Tubes called arteries carry blood from my heart to my other body parts.

Tubes called veins carry the blood back to my heart.

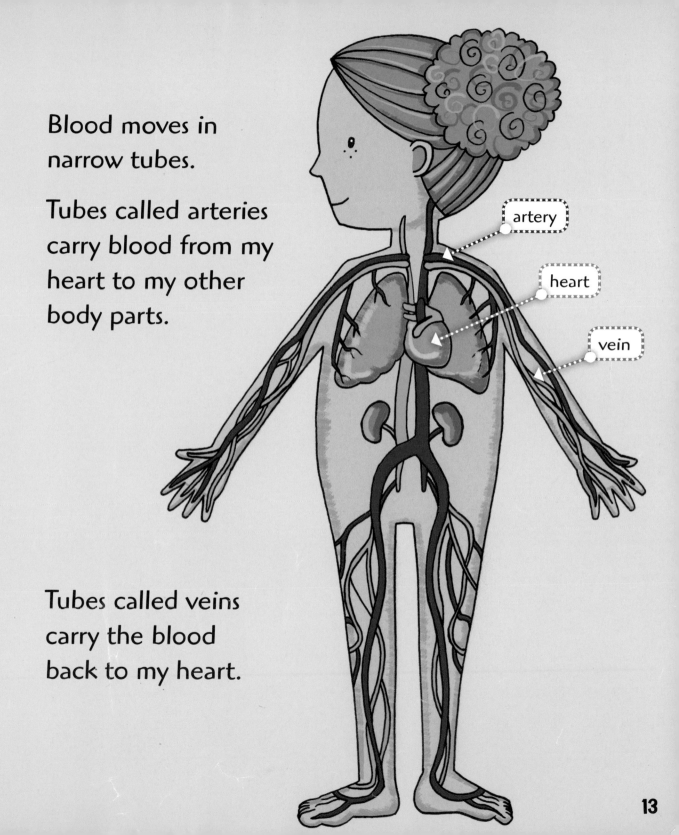

artery

heart

vein

MY LUNGS

My body breathes all the time.

Air goes in my nose to my two lungs.

My lungs take oxygen from the air.

They put the oxygen into my blood.

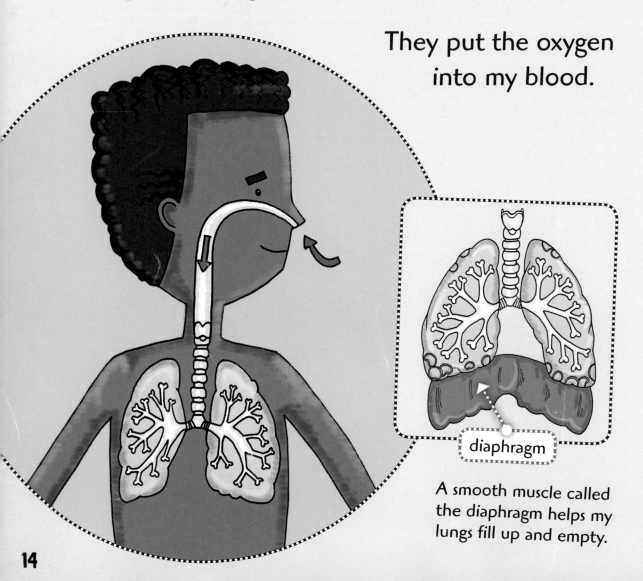

diaphragm

A smooth muscle called the diaphragm helps my lungs fill up and empty.

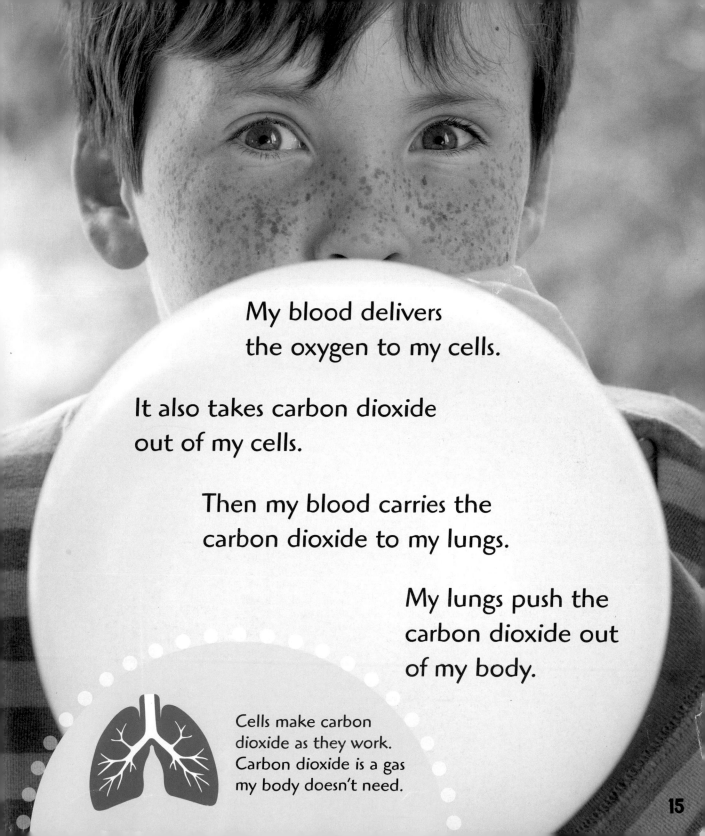

My blood delivers
the oxygen to my cells.

It also takes carbon dioxide
out of my cells.

Then my blood carries the
carbon dioxide to my lungs.

My lungs push the
carbon dioxide out
of my body.

Cells make carbon
dioxide as they work.
Carbon dioxide is a gas
my body doesn't need.

MY HEART

My heart is a muscle.

It works all the time.

My heart pumps blood
through my body.

It squeezes
and relaxes.

This pattern is called
a heartbeat.

MY HEART HAS TWO JOBS.

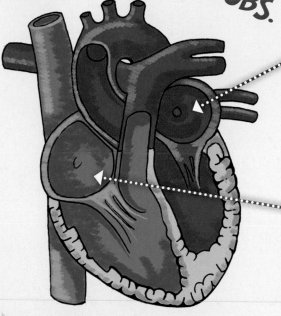

LEFT SIDE
The left side of my heart takes blood from my lungs. It delivers blood with oxygen to my body parts.

RIGHT SIDE
The right side of my heart pumps the blood back to my lungs for more oxygen.

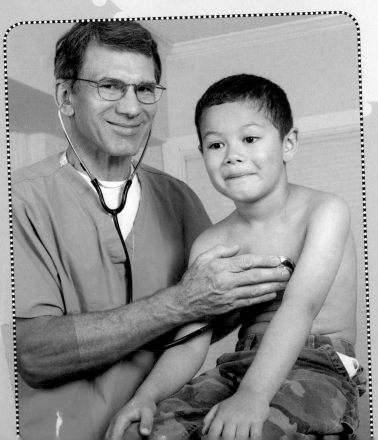

My heart is about the size of my fist.

FIGHTING GERMS

My blood helps keep my body healthy.

White blood cells fight germs that make my body sick.

My blood carries the germs away.

Snot is a sticky liquid called mucus. It helps trap germs before they get into my body.

My skin helps keep my body healthy too.

Skin covers my body and keeps germs out.

It helps keep my body from getting too hot or too cold.

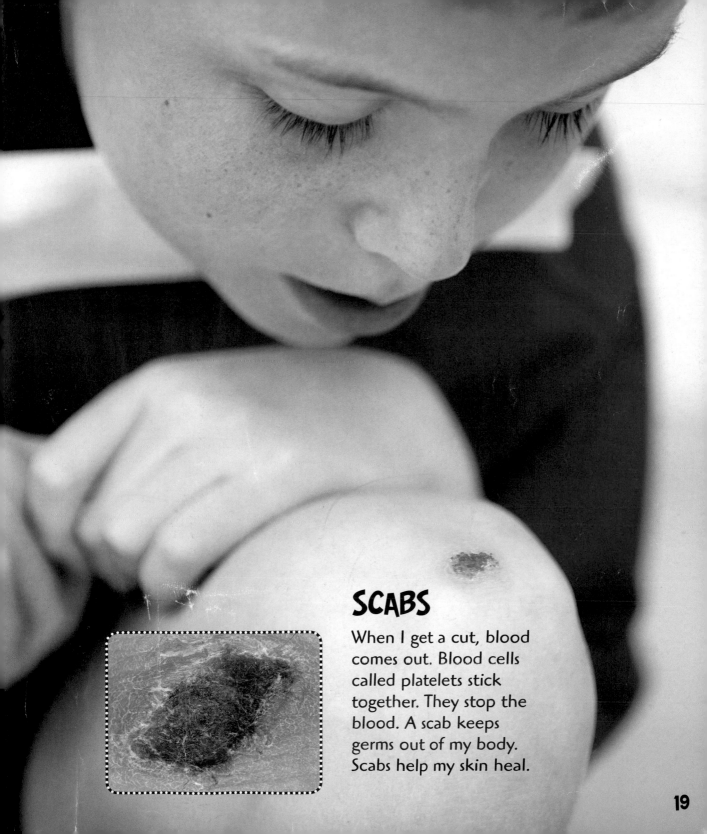

SCABS

When I get a cut, blood comes out. Blood cells called platelets stick together. They stop the blood. A scab keeps germs out of my body. Scabs help my skin heal.

MY BRAIN AND NERVES

My brain helps run my body.

My body gathers information from around me.

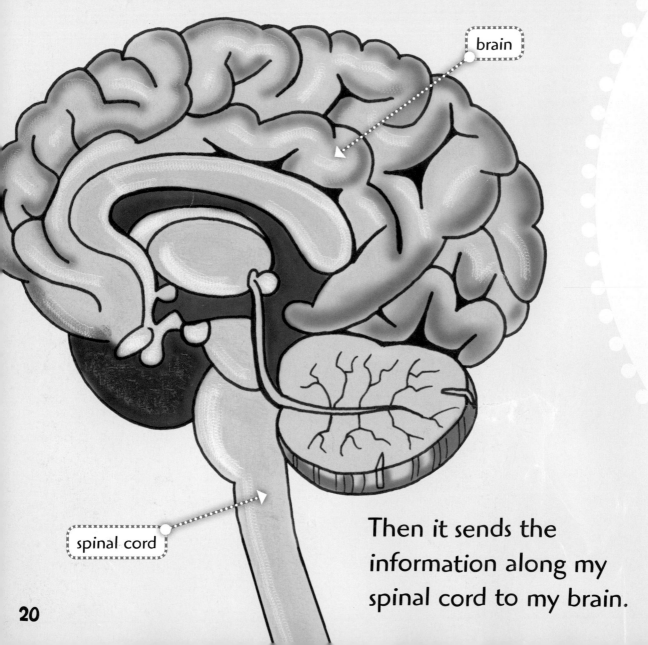

brain

spinal cord

Then it sends the information along my spinal cord to my brain.

Nerves carry messages from my brain to my body parts.

The messages tell my body what to do.

The right half of my brain controls the left side of my body.

The left half of my brain controls the right side of my body.

My spinal cord runs down the middle of my back. The bones of my spine keep it safe.

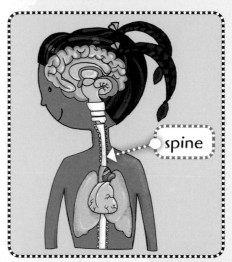

spine

OUCH! THAT'S HOT!

Some important messages are sent right from my spinal cord to my body. This is called a reflex.

MY SENSES

My senses tell my brain a lot.

My skin feels warm sunshine.

My eyes look at the blue sky.

My ears hear birds singing.

My tongue tastes ice cream.

My nose smells cut grass.

My brain tells me it is summer.

OTHER SENSES

My body has more than five senses. My sense of motion tells me where my body is. My sense of balance helps me walk without falling down.

FUELING MY BODY

Food gives my body nutrients and energy.

I chew food with my teeth.

When I swallow, food goes to my stomach.

Spit is also called saliva. It helps break down food in my mouth.

My stomach breaks
food into small parts.

My small intestine
takes the nutrients
from the food that
my body needs.

My large intestine
helps move waste
out of my body.

25

MY GLANDS

Glands help make my body parts work.

Tear glands help my eyes see.

Sweat glands keep my body cool.

Some glands help my body use food to make energy.

Other glands help me grow.

DIABETES

Diabetes is a disease. A gland called the pancreas helps the body use sugar. People who have diabetes sometimes need medicine to help the pancreas do its job.

STAYING HEALTHY

Exercise keeps my muscles strong.

Eating healthy food helps me grow.

Sleep gives my body time to rest.

I take good care of my body.

MY BODY IS AN AMAZING MACHINE!

KIDS SHOULD EXERCISE
60 MINUTES EACH DAY.
—National Institutes of Health

HOW MUCH SLEEP?

AGE	HOURS NEEDED
Babies	16
Kids	10
Adults	8

GLOSSARY

cell—a tiny structure that makes up all living things

energy—the ability to do work

germ—a tiny living thing that causes sickness

gland—an organ in the body that makes certain chemicals

large intestine—a tube that is the last part of the digestive system

microscope—a tool that magnifies very small objects

motion—moving or being moved

nerve—a thin fiber that carries messages between the brain and other parts of the body

nutrient—something that is needed by people, animals, and plants to stay healthy and strong

oxygen—a colorless gas in the air that people need to breathe

reflex—an action that happens without a person's control or effort

small intestine—a long tube between the stomach and the large intestine

CRITICAL THINKING USING THE COMMON CORE

What are some parts of the body that help fight germs? How do they help? (Key Ideas and Details)

How do the photographs on page 4 show that the body is like a machine? (Craft and Structure)

Why do you think you need less sleep as you get older? Do some online research to help answer the question. (Integration of Knowledge and Ideas)

READ MORE

Berger, Gilda and Melvin. *Why Do Feet Smell?: And 20 Answers about the Human Body.* New York: Scholastic, 2012.

Guillain, Charlotte. *How Does My Body Work?* Chicago: Heinemann Library, 2012.

Weber, Rebecca. *How Your Body Works.* Pebble Plus: Health and Your Body. Mankato, Minn.: Capstone Press, 2011.

INTERNET SITES

FactHound offers a safe, fun way to find Internet sites related to this book. All of the sites on FactHound have been researched by our staff.

Here's all you do:

Visit *www.facthound.com*

Type in this code: 9781476502502

INDEX